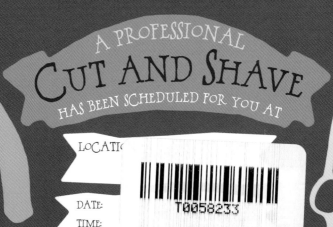

A PROFESSIONAL
CUT AND SHAVE
HAS BEEN SCHEDULED FOR YOU AT

LOCATION:

DATE:

TIME:

T0058233

FOR THE WORLD'S GREATEST DAD

FROM

REDEEM THIS VOUCHER FOR
AN UNEXPECTED
CAKE
AT AN
UNEXPECTED
TIME

FOR THE WORLD'S GREATEST DAD
FROM

FOR THE WORLD'S GREATEST DAD

FROM

LET'S HAVE
A FAMILY
BBQ

FOR THE WORLD'S GREATEST DAD FROM

LET'S TAKE YOU ON A
BOATING
EXCURSION

DATES:

FOR THE WORLD'S GREATEST DAD FROM

FOR THE WORLD'S GREATEST DAD
FROM

FOR THE WORLD'S GREATEST DAD

FROM

GOOD FOR ONE OFFICIAL AND UNCONDITIONAL

WEEKEND PASS

_____

FOR THE WORLD'S GREATEST DAD

FROM

THIS CARD ENTITLES YOU TO

___ TICKETS ~ OF FINEST QUALITY ~ TO:

FOR THE WORLD'S GREATEST DAD

FROM

FOR THE WORLD'S GREATEST DAD
FROM

REDEEM THIS COUPON FOR
A NIGHT OUT ON
THE TOWN

FOR THE WORLD'S GREATEST DAD

FROM

REDEEM THIS COUPON FOR ONE

OUTDOOR ADVENTURE

FOR THE WORLD'S GREATEST DAD

FROM

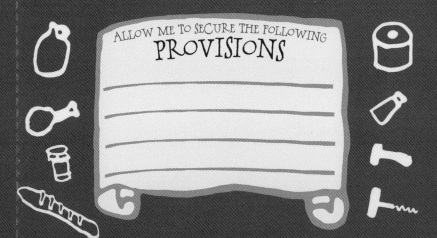

ALLOW ME TO SECURE THE FOLLOWING
PROVISIONS

FOR THE WORLD'S GREATEST DAD

★ FROM ★

USE THIS COUPON FOR:

FOR THE WORLD'S GREATEST DAD

FROM

REDEEM THIS FOR
COMPLAINT-FREE
YARD WORK

FOR THE WORLD'S GREATEST DAD
FROM

WITH THIS CARD WE WILL PRESENT

A HOME-COOKED MEAL TO REMEMBER

STARTER:

MAIN COURSE:

DESSERT:

REDEEM THIS TICKET

FOR AN AFTERNOON

BIKE RIDE

FOR THE WORLD'S GREATEST DAD
FROM

THIS CARD ENTITLES YOU

TO A HANDY

APPRENTICE

DUTIES:

FOR THE WORLD'S GREATEST DAD

FROM

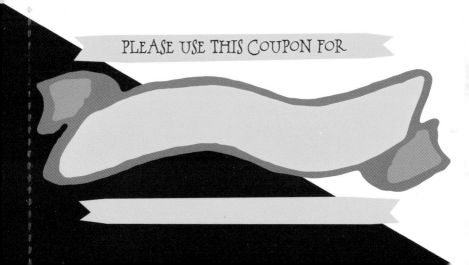

PLEASE USE THIS COUPON FOR

THIS COUPON IS REDEEMABLE FOR

A FUN FAMILY NIGHT IN

FOR THE WORLD'S GREATEST DAD

FROM